CALL ME ROBERTO!

ROBERTO CLEMENTE GOES TO BAT FOR LATINOS

Nathalie Alonso

Art by Rudy Gutierrez

CALKINS CREEK
AN IMPRINT OF ASTRA BOOKS FOR YOUNG READERS
New York

"I was born to be a base[ball]

In the quiet sugar town of Carolina, Puerto Rico, Roberto Clemente is always playing béisbol.
He doesn't care that his ball is a tin can and his bat a tree branch. Or that his field is muddy and cluttered with palmas. Or that his mother, Doña Luisa, has dinner ready.

Roberto lives to swing
and slide.
To catch.
To throw.
To run.

Nineteen-year-old Roberto catches the eye of a scout for a Major League team. With the blessing of his father, Don Melchor, he says adiós to his Caribbean island and travels north. He's going to be a famous pelotero!

But Roberto's first stop is chilly Montreal, where he often sits on the bench, longing to play béisbol.

Finally, on a spring day in 1955, Roberto gets to play in the Major Leagues. In his first at-bat for the Pittsburgh Pirates, he whacks the ball to the left side of the infield, blazes down to first base—*SAFE!*

The next batter hits the ball to right field. At full speed Roberto rounds third base and . . . *SCORES!*

Many Pittsburgh fans love Roberto's bold style, but not everyone is quick to embrace a Black man from Puerto Rico who speaks español.

"I represent the common people of America. So I am going to be treated like a human being."

Roberto hears taunts from opposing players and people in the stands. His teammates keep their distance, and newspaper reporters mock him when he speaks English.

Yet Roberto holds his head up high as he swings and slides . . .

. . . And runs!
Roberto motors around the bases with an inside-the-park grand slam in one game, three triples in another. The Pirates' radio announcer starts chanting "¡Arriba! ¡Arriba!" when Roberto is at the plate.

. . . And catches and throws!
Out in right field, Roberto is an acrobat. He leaps and dives and reaches over the wall to rob hits and home runs. And base runners don't stand a chance against his powerful right arm.

But newspaper reporters don't praise Roberto's energy: They call him a show-off. And when his back hurts and he can't play, lazy! To make things worse, people call him "Bob." They think it sounds more familiar—more American.

Roberto doesn't like being called Bob.
   Call me Roberto, he insists, orgulloso to be from Puerto Rico.
   And Puerto Rico is just as proud of him.

In 1960 Roberto is an All-Star for the first time, and he's hitting the ball farther than ever. Sixteen of those balls clear the fence . . . GONE!

Roberto's 16 home runs and 94 runs batted in propel the Pirates to the World Series. Doña Luisa travels to Pittsburgh to see him play, while the rest of Puerto Rico is glued to the radio.

On baseball's biggest stage, Roberto shines. In his first World Series at-bat, he ropes a single to center field, driving in a run as the Pirates take Game 1. In a decisive Game 7, Roberto's infield hit pushes a run across the plate and . . .

. . . The Pirates win 10–9. They are champions of baseball!

Roberto is the only Pirates' player with a hit in every World Series game. Yet few people in Pittsburgh seem to notice. While the Pirates celebrate, the boy from Carolina heads home to his beloved island, where fans sounding pitos and tambores give him a hero's welcome.

"If I'm good enough to play here, I have to be good enough to be treated like the rest of the players."

PIRATES WORLD CHAMPS!

Puerto Rico throws party after party for Roberto. But he yearns to be recognized in Pittsburgh, too. When the newspaper reporters vote him eighth for the Most Valuable Player Award, Roberto is outraged.

They won't acknowledge his talent.
Because he is Black.
Because he is Puerto Rican.
And it's not the only injustice he faces.

In Puerto Rico, Roberto is free to go wherever he wants. But in segregated Florida, where the Pirates train each spring, the team hotel and most other places are off-limits for a Black man—even a World Series champion.

While his White teammates play golf and swim at the beach, Roberto is stuck in his room in another part of town. "It's like being in prison," he tells a reporter.

Roberto continues to demand justice for himself and for players like him. But it's on the field that he makes himself heard.

A determined Roberto has his best season yet. At the 1961 All-Star Game, with the score tied, he smacks the ball to right field—A GAME-WINNING SINGLE!

When the season is over, Roberto leads his league with a .351 batting average and wins a Gold Glove for his spectacular catches and throws.

There is no ignoring Roberto now. The ball is flying off his bat! He hits 29 home runs and drives in 119 runs for the Pirates in 1966.

At the end of the season, the newspaper writers can't deny it: Roberto is the MVP. El más valioso. By now, more players from places where palmas grow and people speak español are shining in the Major Leagues.

Roberto's hard work is paying off, but the biggest performance of his career is yet to come . . .

When the Pirates make it back to the World Series in 1971, Roberto once again has a hit in every game. In Game 7, he wallops a home run to left field to help the Pirates win 2–1.

The Pirates are champions again! And this time, Roberto is named MVP of the World Series—a first for a Spanish-speaking player.

Puerto Ricans beam as Roberto asks Doña Luisa and Don Melchor for their blessing on television en español. And he is not done making his people proud.

"En el día más grande de mi vida, para los nenes la bendición mía, y que mis padres me echen mi bendición en Puerto Rico".

On a September afternoon, Roberto clobbers a ball to left field for a double—HIS 3,000TH HIT! Few players have ever had that many hits in the Major Leagues.

Standing tall on second base, the boy from Carolina tips his helmet to the crowd. After 18 seasons, he still lives to swing and slide.

And to catch.

And to throw.

And to run.

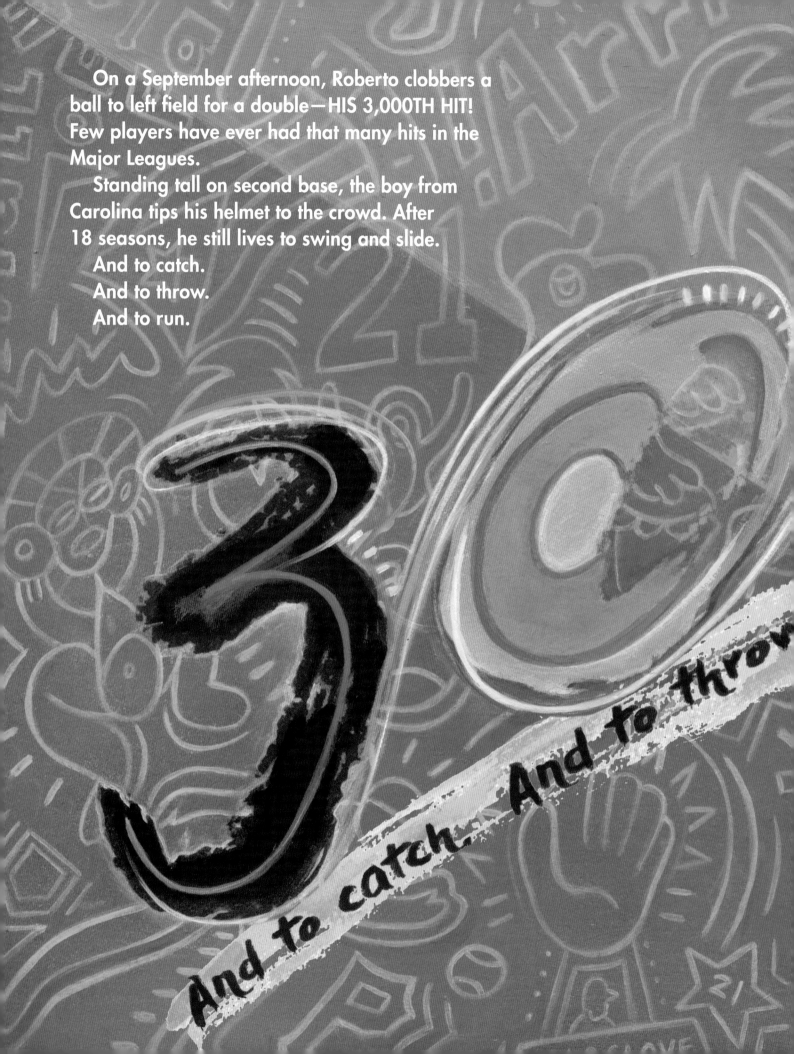

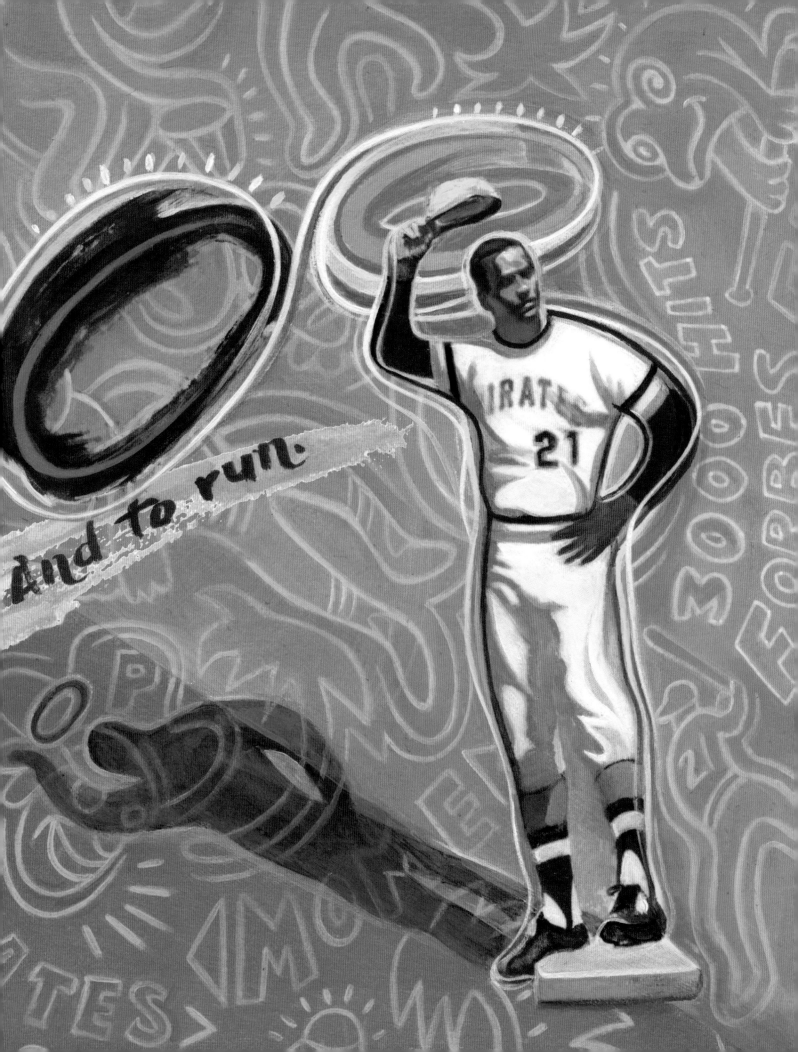

Author's Note

On December 31, 1972, three months after collecting his 3,000th hit, thirty-eight-year-old Roberto Clemente boarded a plane in San Juan, Puerto Rico. He was on his way to deliver supplies to earthquake victims in Nicaragua. The aircraft crashed into the ocean shortly after takeoff, claiming the lives of everyone on board.

Because of the circumstances of his death Roberto has long been honored primarily as a humanitarian figure. And while he certainly deserves to be recognized as such, that narrative has obscured what I see as his greatest contribution to baseball: his battle to get the sport to accept and embrace players from Latin America. It is this legacy that most resonates with me as a first-generation Latina who covers baseball for a living, a job that has traditionally been the domain of White men.

I was twenty when I started my journalism career at MLB.com, writing, translating, and producing stories for a Spanish-language audience. I have since covered players, coaches, and managers who hail from Roberto's native Puerto Rico, my mother's native Cuba, as well as the Dominican Republic, Venezuela, and other Latin American countries. Many of those players rank among the game's biggest and most beloved stars.

But when Roberto arrived in the Majors, he encountered an industry that, years after Jackie Robinson's debut with the Dodgers, remained hostile to people of color. Early on in his career, newspapers mocked Roberto's Puerto Rican accent by quoting him using phonetic spelling. When physical ailments kept him off the field, reporters call him a hypochondriac and accused him of being lazy. And when he complained about this treatment, the media dismissed him as a malcontent. As an Afro-Puerto Rican man, Roberto was also subject to Jim Crow laws.

Yet Roberto, who identified with the Civil Rights Movement—the African American struggle for equality—remained fiercely and unapologetically proud of his roots. His refusal to bow to bigotry and his defiance of racist stereotypes are what most inspire me. As someone whose first language is Spanish but who wasn't always comfortable speaking it in professional settings, the moment when Roberto addressed his parents on national television is incredibly validating.

Roberto, of course, ranks among the most accomplished players of all time. In 18 seasons with the Pirates, he hit .317, clobbered 240 home runs and drove in 1,305 runs, while claiming four batting titles and 12 Gold Gloves and making 15 All-Star Game appearances. He was the 1966 National League MVP and helped Pittsburgh win the World Series twice. After his death, he was inducted into the National Baseball Hall of Fame. Major League Baseball has designated September 15 as Roberto Clemente Day, and each year the league awards the Roberto Clemente Award to an active player who embodies his values.

It is important to note that Roberto was not the first Afro-Latino player to suit up for an American or National League team. That distinction belongs to the Cuban-born Orestes "Minnie" Miñoso, a major figure in the integration of baseball who faced the same hostility. By continuing the legacy of Miñoso and others, Roberto helped clear a path for players from Latin America to star in the Major Leagues—and for a reporter like me to cover them. The players and coaches whose stories I tell see themselves in Roberto Clemente. He is their hero. And mine.

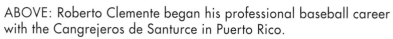

ABOVE: Roberto Clemente began his professional baseball career with the Cangrejeros de Santurce in Puerto Rico.

RIGHT: In addition to his prowess at the plate, Roberto Clemente was known for his spectacular defense in right field.

Roberto Clemente played his entire 18-year Major League career with the Pittsburgh Pirates.

Glossary

adiós: goodbye

arriba: up, or when doubled it serves as an expression

béisbol: baseball

Don/Doña: titles of respect for older individuals

el más valioso: the most valuable

en español: in Spanish

orgulloso: proud

palmas: palm trees

pelotero: ball player

pitos: whistles

tambores: drums

Translation of Quotation
(page 30)

On the biggest day of my life, I give my blessing to my kids and (ask) that my parents give me their blessing in Puerto Rico.

Timeline of Roberto Clemente's Life

Aug. 18, 1934: Roberto Enrique Clemente Walker is born in Carolina, Puerto Rico.

Oct. 9, 1952: Roberto signs with the Cangrejeros de Santurce baseball team of the Puerto Rican Winter League.

Feb. 19, 1954: Roberto signs with the Brooklyn Dodgers.

Nov. 22, 1954: The Pittsburgh Pirates select Roberto from the Brooklyn Dodgers in the Rule 5 Draft.

April 17, 1955: Roberto makes his Major League debut with the Pirates.

1958: Roberto joins the US Marine Corps Reserve.

1960: The Pittsburgh Pirates beat the New York Yankees in the World Series. Roberto finishes eighth in National League Most Valuable Player voting.

1961: Roberto wins the first of twelve consecutive Gold Gloves and earns his first National League batting title after finishing the season with a .351 average.

Nov. 14, 1964: Roberto marries Vera Cristina Zabala in San Juan, Puerto Rico. The marriage produces three sons: Roberto Jr., Luis Roberto, and Enrique Roberto.

1966: After what is considered his best season, Roberto is named National League MVP.

Sept. 1, 1971: With Roberto in right field, the Pirates field what is believed to be the first all-Black and Latino lineup in Major League history.

Oct. 17, 1971: The Pirates beat the Baltimore Orioles in the World Series. Roberto is the World Series MVP.

Sept. 30, 1972: Roberto doubles in his last game of the 1972 regular season to reach 3,000 hits. He is the first Latino and the 11th player in Major League history to reach that milestone.

Dec. 31, 1972: The plane Roberto charters to deliver supplies to earthquake-ravaged Nicaragua crashes into the ocean shortly after takeoff. There are no survivors.

Aug. 6, 1973: Roberto becomes the first Latin American player inducted into the National Baseball Hall of Fame.

Selected Bibliography

All quotations used in the book can be found in the following sources marked with an asterisk (*).

Abrams, Al. "Sidelight on Sports: A Baseball Star is Born." *Pittsburgh Post-Gazette*, June 7, 1995, 20.

Beschloss, Michael. "Clemente, the Double Outsider." *New York Times*, June 19, 2015. nytimes.com/2015/06/20/upshot/clemente-the-double-outsider.html.

Berkow, Ira. "Maybe They'll Understand Clemente Now." *Nevada Daily Mail*, Nov. 2, 1971, 11.

Beyond Baseball: The Life of Roberto Clemente. 2007–2012, Smithsonian Institution Traveling Exhibition Services.

Biederman, Les. "Hitting in Daylight (.411 Versus .302) Best for Clemente." *Pittsburgh Press*, March 11, 1962, sec. 4, 3.

The Clemente Family. *Clemente: The True Legacy of an Undying Hero*. New York: Celebra, 2013.

"Clemente Unsung Hero of Series." *Decatur Daily Review*, Oct. 11, 1960, 15.

* "A Conversation with Roberto Clemente." Sam Nover, WICC-TV, Oct. 8, 1972.

Cope, Myron. "Aches and Pains and Three Batting Titles." *Sports Illustrated*, Mar. 7, 1966, 30–40.

* Maraniss, David. *Clemente: The Passion and Grace of Baseball's Last Hero*. New York: Simon & Schuster, 2007.

——. "No Gentle Saint." *The Undefeated*, July 15, 2016. theundefeated.com/features/roberto-clemente-was-a-fierce-critic-of-both-baseball-and-american-society.

Nunn Jr., Bill. "Change of Pace." *Pittsburgh Courier*, May 7, 1960, 26.

Prato, Lou. "Clemente Will Seek Raise in Pay Next Year." *Gettysburg Times*, Oct. 3, 1961, 5.

Schuyler Jr., Ed. "Clemente Unorthodox? Well, He Gets Results." *Daytona Beach Morning Journal*, Aug. 11, 1964, 7.

Walker, Paul Robert. *Pride of Puerto Rico: The Life of Roberto Clemente*. New York: Harcourt Brace Jovanovich, 1991.

Ways, C. R. "Nobody Does Anything Better Than Me in Baseball, Says Roberto Clemente." *New York Times Magazine*, April 9, 1972, 38–48.

Acknowledgments

It's hard to imagine that *Call Me Roberto!* would be out in the world without the support I received from the Highlights Foundation's Diversity Fellowship in Children's Literature. I am forever indebted to George Brown and Alison Green Myers for giving me the resources to make the leap from journalist to children's author.

Sincerest gratitude to Leah Henderson, who saw my potential to write for children long before I did, and to my Fellowship mentor and friend Emma Otheguy, for her insightful notes on the earliest drafts of this book. I'd also like to acknowledge Harold Underdown and Eileen Robinson, whose revision workshop helped me figure out the voice and direction for this story, and Rona Shirdan, whose eye for detail always makes my writing better. And, I am grateful for the conversations about Roberto Clemente that I've had with Professor Adrian Burgos, Jr., which have helped shape my understanding of Roberto's legacy.

I found myself in a position to write this book because Suzanne Medina gave me the opportunity to work in baseball. Forever grateful to her for hiring me for my dream job and for the encouragement I've received from all of my colleagues at LasMayores.com.

I am fortunate to have had an amazing support group to lean on while working on this book, starting with my fellow Diversity Fellows: Adriana De Persia Colón, Pamela Courtney, Krystal Song, Daria Peoples, Jacqueline Barnes, Narmeen Lakhani, Trisha Tobias, Gerry Himmelreich, and Jessica Galán. Thank you for your love, feedback, and encouragement. Many thanks also to my friend and fellow writer Sydney Bergman for cheering me on throughout the process.

And to my editor, Carolyn Yoder, and my agent, Heather Cashman—thank you not only for believing that Roberto Clemente's story deserves to be told, but for trusting that I am the right person to tell it.

Illustrator's Note

Roberto Clemente for me represents beauty, grace, dignity, divinity, social responsibility, poetry in motion, and of course love for our Puerto Rican souls and beyond. He is the best of us and it is an honor to conjure him with my art with the hope that I can do him justice by inspiring others to know their glorious validity!

—RG

Picture Credits

To my mother, for always taking me to the library —*NA*

For all of those who love their heritage and dare to
walk their path towards who they are! —*RG*

Calkins Creek
An imprint of Astra Books for Young Readers,
a division of Astra Publishing House
astrapublishinghouse.com
Printed in China

ISBN: 978-1-63592-811-2 (hc)
ISBN: 978-1-63592-812-9 (eBook)
Library of Congress Control Number: 2023914428

First edition
10 9 8 7 6 5 4 3 2 1

Design by Barbara Grzeslo
The text is set in Futura Std Medium.
The illustrations are done in mixed media—acrylic paint with colored pencils and crayons.